LSWR Class L12 4-4-0 No 419, one of 20 built to Drummond's design in 1904-5, heads a Waterloo-Exeter express past Clapham Cutting signal box around 1910. /*Painting by G. F. Heiron*

London & South Western Railway Album

London & South Western Railway Album

D. L. Bradley

LONDON
IAN ALLAN LTD

First published 1976

ISBN 0 7110 0744 6

Published by Ian Allan Ltd, Shepperton, Surrey, and printed in the United Kingdom by Ian Allan Printing Ltd.

INTRODUCTION

To the railway historian the attraction of the pre-Grouping companies undoubtedly lay in their individuality, with exponents of the various railways invariably striving to project those features peculiar to their own particular line. In this the London & South Western Railway's task was greatly simplified by a Locomotive Department whose every facet from 1850 until Grouping personified individualism. In the early years there were the coal-burning fireboxes and feedwater heaters of Joseph Beattie, at mid-life the inspection car and double-singles of Dugald Drummond and at Grouping the robust simplicity of Robert Urie.

The London & South Western originated as the London & Southampton Railway on 25 July 1834, when Parliament authorised a line from London to Southampton via Wimbledon, Woking, Basingstoke and Winchester with a capital of £1,000,000 and loans of a further £330,000. Under the forceful and astute direction of Joseph Locke the works proceeded apace, with the opening throughout being made on 11 May 1840. The 77 mile journey to Southampton was performed in a little over 3hr by first-class trains and in 6¼hr by mixed or goods services, most creditable performances for the period.

A further approach to Parliament on 4 June 1839 gained authority for the construction of a branch line from Bishopstoke (later known as Eastleigh) to Gosport, with the intention of serving the naval city of Portsmouth by means of a ferry. This Act also empowered a change of title to the more logical London & South Western Railway. In later years, however, it appears that the Directors would have preferred a simpler style for most public notices and timetables, as some locomotives and the front of old Waterloo station were lettered South Western Railway.

Over the next few years other lines were constructed from Basingstoke to Salisbury, Southampton to Dorchester and Woking to Guildford, while later came extensions to Portsmouth, Bournemouth via Sway and in the West Country to Exeter, Ilfracombe, Torrington, Bude, Padstow and Plymouth. Various other cross-country and branch lines were opened until the company offered the inhabitants of Wessex one of the most comprehensive train services in the country. Serious attention was also given to the London area, where strategically sited stations and lines ensured an ever-increasing flow of commuters through the terminus at Waterloo.

Passenger traffic always played an important role and in time led to the development of Bournemouth from a fishing hamlet at the mouth of the river Bourne to a holiday resort rivalling Brighton in hotel accommodation and amenities. The improved means of transport also made it possible for farmers and market gardeners to reach London with their produce in prime condition. In particular this applied to milk, with the South Western operating an extensive service of van trains to passenger timings seven days a week. Fresh vegetables also gained importance while in season strawberries, raspberries, blackcurrants and watercress were despatched by the trainload not only to Covent Garden, but also to the Midlands and North.

From 1850 until 1871 the Locomotive Department was ruled by Joseph Beattie, who had received his engineering training on the Grand Junction Railway under Joseph Locke. At the time of his appointment all South Western express services were worked by singles, but after adding a small class of his own, Beattie appreciated the need of greater power and transferred his allegiance to 2-4-0s. These, with wheel diameters of five to seven feet, covered all main line requirements, except the heaviest goods, while a neat tank version was charged with the London suburban and branch line services. All were equipped with patent coal-burning fireboxes, donkey pumps and feedwater heaters, the latter often having the appearance of auxiliary chimneys. Like many top men of his era, Joseph Beattie was an insatiable worker; with advance into late middle age his constitution faltered and death came suddenly in October 1871.

History offers few instances of celebrated fathers being succeeded by equally renowned sons, and William George Beattie evinced little to disprove the theory when appointed mechanical engineer in November 1871. As long as he perpetuated his father's designs all remained well, but when he branched out for himself, such trouble beset the South Western that his resignation was requested in December 1877.

As a replacement the South Western was fortunate to gain that giant of Victorian locomotive engineers, William Adams. There was an urgent need of larger and more powerful locomotives for both goods and passenger services, and to this end the new chief rapidly introduced 6ft 7in and 7ft 1in express 4-4-0s, six-coupled goods and 4-4-2 tanks for branch and suburban service. All proved eminently successful and, with their robust construction, generous bearing surfaces and free steaming boilers, proved an absolute godsend to the severely taxed Locomotive Department.

Later these classes were followed by more advanced 4-4-0s, the mixed traffic 'Jubilees', yard and dock shunters, and large and small 0-4-4 tanks. These also gave excellent service and when painted in the attractive Adams apple green livery were amongst the best looking locomotives in the country. Apart from the necessity of adding trailing wheels to his early suburban tanks, Adams built no unsatisfactory locomotives for the South Western before ill-health forced his retirement in July 1895.

As was to be expected, such a man proved most difficult to replace and it is likely that whoever came to Nine Elms would have been resented by his many friends and colleagues. Under these conditions, it is hard to imagine anyone more likely to rip the entire Locomotive Department asunder than the Directors' choice, Dugald Drummond. When he took office in August 1895, the Department was not left long in doubt that it had caught a real tartar. Within days he had cast aside all the once highly prized principles of friendliness and co-operation, and soon there arose many instances of long-serving employees tendering their resignation or requesting premature retirement. However, those possessing the strength of mind to withstand the wind of change found that the Drummond bark was considerably harsher than his bite, and that in reality the company had gained the services of an extremely able and venturesome engineer.

Fortunately, Adams had left the South Western well-stocked with locomotives so Drummond could carefully assess the future requirements of his Department before designing classes of his own. For express service, after a brief experimentation with double-singles, he relied on 4-4-0s of similar design to those built earlier for the North British and Caledonian Railways. These he progressively increased in size and power until 1906, when 4-6-0s were introduced for the heavy West of England expresses. Complete success, however, proved most elusive, and although time and experience overcame many of the design failings the Drummond six-coupled classes never gained the same acclaim as his 4-4-0s. Indeed, just prior to his death in 1912, he returned to the four-coupled type for the best Bournemouth trains.

For goods service reliance was placed on 0-6-0s, although an eight-coupled class was considered while powerful 0-4-4 tanks were built for suburban and secondary main line duties. There was also a sizeable number of mixed traffic 4-4-0s for light goods, van and excursion work. Once again the Directors and shareholders were well served by their locomotive engineer since, in addition to keeping ahead of current Running Department requirements, Drummond planned, supervised and opened the new repair shops at Eastleigh.

When forced in December 1912 to appoint a successor, the Directors gave some thought to an outsider, but after careful consideration, offered the post to Robert Urie, their works manager at Eastleigh. He was a firm advocate of simplicity and ease of maintenance, and at once introduced a series of robust two-cylinder 4-6-0s for mixed traffic duty. These he followed by similar locomotives for express passenger and heavy goods service, while large 4-8-0 and 4-6-2 tanks were made available for yard shunting and short-distance goods work. All were superheated since, unlike Drummond, Urie fully understood the fuel and water economy this refinement made possible.

Although dedicated to steam, Urie nevertheless appreciated that a more flexible means of motive power was necessary in and around London to compete with the extensive tramway system. Electricity was the answer and in October 1915 electric services commenced operating between Waterloo and East Putney. Success was immediate and in the years before Grouping extensions were made to Shepperton, Hounslow, Hampton Court and Claygate. Time proved the equipment so efficient and economical that after Grouping the Southern Railway not only extended operations, but introduced similar propulsion on lines previously managed by the South Eastern & Chatham and London Brighton & South Coast Railways.

In the early years the passenger coaches were spacious, well-appointed and comfortable, but later construction failed to keep abreast of that provided by the Great Western and Midland Railways. Much adverse criticism was received, especially from West of England passengers, although apparently with little effect until the 1890s, when an extensive building programme under William Panter gave the South Western a plentiful supply of excellent bogie coaches. Lighting was by electricity, while after the turn of the century steam heating became general in the winter months. Later under the guidance of Surrey Warner came further improvements until at Grouping South Western coaches were comparable with the best in the country.

The majority of the open and covered wagon stock was designed for general merchandise, although there were many fruit, milk and refrigeration vans. The last mentioned were intended for the Southampton Docks-Smithfield meat traffic, while a series of heated vans similarly catered for the West Indies banana trade. There were also a number of specialised vehicles for the conveyance of gold bullion, hides, stone ballast, timber, oil, explosives and bricks.

Civil engineering structures, including some notable tunnels, abounded on the South Western. Most impressive was the lofty and graceful Meldon Viaduct of the Exeter-Plymouth line skirting Dartmoor. The company was, however, spasmodic in providing good passenger stations. Indeed, for many years even the terminus at Waterloo added little to the South Western's image or prestige. Generally the buildings lacked beauty and comfort, though they were often admirably adapted to their traffic. Some, like Exeter Queen Street, were totally inadequate while Bournemouth Central, Portsmouth Town and Southampton Docks were designed and operated with the Running Department in mind rather than the unfortunate traveller. Cleanliness was the sole saving grace; all buildings both inside and out were well maintained and regularly redecorated, while most enjoyed the benefit of electric lighting and excellent plumbing.

The company did not venture extensively into the hotel trade. Its South Western Hotel adjoining Southampton Docks was well managed and adequate, but not exceptional with view to the high potentiality of the ocean liner cross-channel trade, nor was it advertised with verve.

The Directors, however, quickly appreciated the possibility of goods and passenger traffic with the Continent and Channel Islands. Well-found, reliable and fast steamers were built for these services which, if not graced with such fine lines as those operated by the Great Western, were more comfortable and better manned.

Unfortunately similar success did not follow the company's entry into road transport during 1904-5, when services were operated from Exeter, Farnham, Lyndhurst, Lymington and Totton. Steam and motor vehicles were employed, but running costs were high and the First World War offered a reasonable excuse for a graceful withdrawal. Like most large institutions, the London & South Western Railway had its failings, but these were few and had little effect on the excellent service offered to the travellers and merchants of Wessex. It was a truly great railway, the only one to be found in Southern England.

BEATTIE

LOCOMOTIVES

Top left: The earliest London & South Western locomotive known to have been photographed, No 8 *Vesta* built by Sharp, Roberts & Co in August 1838./*Dorset Museum*

Centre left: 'Mazeppa' class No 57 *Meteor*, one of ten 6ft 6in singles constructed at Nine Elms Works in 1847 for the Southampton services.

Bottom left: Costing £1,900 when delivered in 1849, No 114 *Frome* came from the Thames Bank Iron Works of Christie, Adams & Hill.

Above: Many standard Beattie features are present in this view of 'Saxon' class 5ft 2-4-0 No 128 *Samson*, taken at Exmouth in March 1873./*J B N Ashford*

Below: 'Hercules' class 2-4-0 goods No 40 *Windsor* of 1852. Note inside cylinders, slender coupling rods, minute spectacle plate, padded buffers and four-wheeled tender./*Dorset Museum*

Above: Only twelve express singles were built by Joseph Beattie, the last being No 153 *Victoria* in June 1859; it is pictured here at Nine Elms in September 1884/*Ian Allan Library*

Below: 'Undine' class 6ft 6in 2-4-0 No 167 *Atalanta* of 1859 with early pattern Beattie feedwater heater and splasher nameplates.

Above: In its final form the Beattie feedwater system consisted of concentric pipes running along the boiler, these being present on No 84 *Styx*, photographed at Exeter in 1867.

Below: Built with 6ft driving wheels for the sharply graded Salisbury-Exeter line in 1862, No 30 *Vulture* has the intermediate pattern feedwater heater with "pup" chimney and boiler barrel nameplates.

Below: 'Vesuvius' class 6ft 6in 2-4-0 No 294 in September 1894 with the feedwater heating equipment removed and carrying an Adams chimney.

Right: 7ft 0in 2-4-0 No 0100 *Python*, resplendent in Drummond livery and fitted with a Beyer Peacock goods boiler, stands at Salisbury in July 1897. */J B N Ashford*

S W R
PYTHON

294

N-17

Above left: Photographs of Beattie engines on trains are rare, therefore this view of 2-4-0 No 18 approaching Clapham Junction is of particular interest. /*Loco & General*

Above: **Only two of the 6ft 2-4-0s were rebuilt, this picture of No 116 being the only one known to exist./*Author's Collection***

Left: Several of the 6ft 6in 2-4-0s were rebuilt by Adams, including 'Vesuvius' class No 279, seen here at Nine Elms in March 1896.

TARTAR

0196

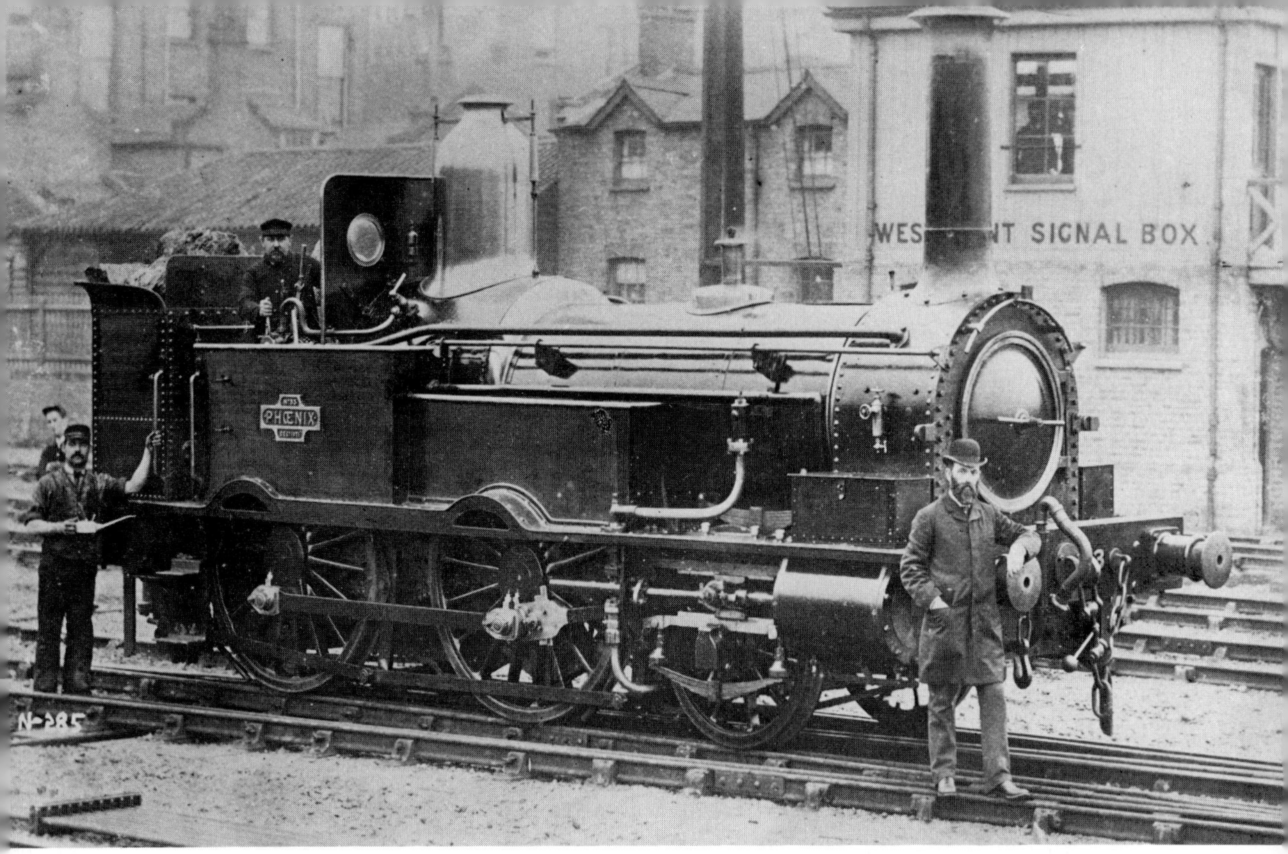

Top left: Chard Junction in May 1872 with 2-2-2 well tank No 13 *Orion* in charge of the branch train. /*Author's Collection*

Centre left: Single-wheel well tank No 2 *Tartar*. Like No 13 *Orion*, it was supplied by Sharp Brothers in 1852.

Below left: 2-4-0 No 0196, an Adams 1884 rebuild of a Beattie well tank.

Above: Singles rapidly lost favour on the South Western and by 1856 four-coupled well tanks were being built. Here No 33 *Phoenix* stands before the West Joint signalbox, Wimbledon in 1882.

Right: Well tank No 248 was sent to work on the isolated Bodmin-Wadebridge line in 1893, hence the cab to offer crews some protection from the elements./*Loco & General*

Above: Nine Elms yard in October 1899 with a group of shunters posed before Adams reboilered No 0329.

Below: 'Lion' class 0-6-0 No 53 at Exeter in March 1867. This was the standard Beattie goods built at Nine Elms from 1865 to 1873.

Top right: Standing in Milford yard, No 274 was one of 24 double-frame 0-6-0s supplied by Beyer Peacock & Co concurrently with the Nine Elms 'Lion' class.

Centre right: Petersfield in October 1908 with double-frame 0-6-0 No 0287 approaching with a pick-up goods./*Author's collection*

Bottom right: Double-frame goods No 277 in April 1896 with Adams boiler, cab and stove pipe chimney.

Above: Further 0-6-0s were ordered by W G Beattie from Beyer Peacock & Co in 1874-8 but these, like No 345 pictured at Templecombe, had inside frames.

Below: Adams reboilered single-frame goods No 347 shunting the east yard at Bournemouth Central in May 1901./*C H Eden*

Top right: In 1873-80, eight light 0-6-0s were purchased from Beyer Peacock & Co for the Exeter-Ilfracombe services. No 0394 of the final series awaits repair at Nine Elms in February 1903./*C H Eden*

Centre right: Ilfracombe goods No 0282, with an Adams boiler and a six-wheeled Beyer Peacock tender, stands on Nine Elms shed in April 1899. /*Author's collection*

Bottom right: 330 class six-coupled saddle tank No 413, another standard Beyer Peacock design to find favour on the South Western.

0394

0282
L S W R

413
S W R

0319

358

Top left: Metropolitan Tank No 322 with a train of Great Western stock leaving Winchester Chesil for Southampton in August 1900./*Loco & General*

Centre left: Displaying evidence of its recent relegation to Duplicate Stock, Metropolitan Tank No 0319 acts as carriage pilot at Bournemouth West in September 1900./C H Eden

Bottom left: Reasonable success as Locomotive Superintendent was achieved by W G Beattie until the delivery of twenty express 4-4-0s by Sharp, Stewart & Co in 1877. Numbered 348 to 367, they failed so dismally that the Directors demanded his resignation./*Mitchell Library*

Above: 348 class No 0353 at Bournemouth Central in April 1902 after rebuilding with Adams boiler, cylinders, cab, chimney, and tender./*C H Eden*

Below: On the same day No 0353 leaves Bournemouth Central with a stopping train for Weymouth./*C H Eden*

STATIONS

Above: The station, goods yard and engine shed at Yeovil Town in July 1886 with one of the Beyer Peacock single-frame 0-6-0s in the foreground. /*Loco & General*

Below: Looking west at Bournemouth Central in June 1903. The 800ft platforms are partially enclosed by a glass canopy 40ft above rail level, 350ft in length and spanning 95ft./*C H Eden*

Top right: Eggesford on the Barnstaple and Yeoford line with a standard-gauge Great Western goods train approaching./*Loco & General*

Centre right: Drummond steam railcar about to leave Bishops Waltham for Botley in July 1907. /*British Railways*

Bottom right: The 7.50 to Waterloo, headed by Adams radial tank No 484, stopping at Feltham in May 1908./*Author's collection*

SUTTON'S SEEDS

Above: The new Waterloo in May 1913 with 'Paddlebox' No 446 leaving for Bournemouth with the 4.10pm express./*LCGB*

Below: A typical South Western wayside station — Liphook, between Haslemere and Liss. /*Author's collection*

Above right: Southampton West in April 1922 with the elegant clock tower overshadowing superheated D15 class No 463./*H C Casserley*

Below right: The South Western's terminus at Plymouth in July 1923 with T1 class No 72 about to depart for St Budeaux./*H C Casserley*

463

LOCO DEPT
No 1
NINE ELMS
79

ENGINEER'S DEPARTMENT

Left: Unlike most railways, the South Western until 1888 maintained a separate stock of Engineer's Department locomotives. Most were ungainly long-boiler George England 2-4-0s similar to No 6, *Telford./Author's collection*

Below left: Breakdown crane No 1 at Nine Elms in April 1919. Built at Bath by Stothert & Pitt Ltd in 1908, it had a 20ton lift./*Ian Allan Library*

Above: Purchased from George England in 1861, No 021 *Scott* had a long and varied career which included shunting the Wimbledon permanent way depot, working on the Bodmin & Wadebridge Railway and carriage-piloting at Clapham Junction.

Below: No 148 *Colne* came from the Somerset & Dorset Railway in 1878, was transferred to the Engineer's Department as No 3 *Stephenson* in 1884 and withdrawn in 1889./*Ian Allan Library*

COACHING STOCK

Left: Non-corridor bogie third No 513, one of a numerous series introduced by W Panter at a cost of £670 in 1898./*British Railways*

Below left: Six-wheeled family-picnic saloon No 4, a 1900 conversion of an 1878 composite coach. /*British Railways*

Bottom left: Surrey Warner ordered four sleeping cars at £1,400 each for the Plymouth services in 1907. Entering traffic the following year, they were little used and were sold to the Great Western./*British Railways*

Right: The interior of sleeping car No 42, showing the movable brass-headed bed, collapsible table and electric lighting./*British Railways*

Below: The sumptuous interior of saloon No 4. /*British Railways*

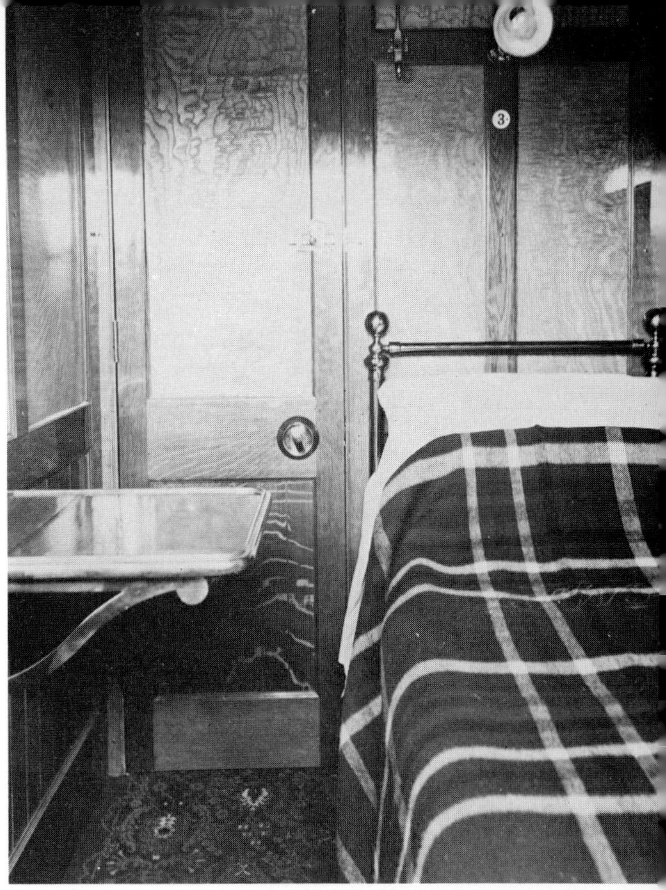

Above: The West of England milk traffic demanded many vans, although few were as elegant and modern as salmon-liveried No 163./*Author's collection*

Below: Vestibule Parlour Car *Duchess of Fife* at Bournemouth Central July 1901, about to leave on the 2.07pm express to Waterloo./*C H Eden*

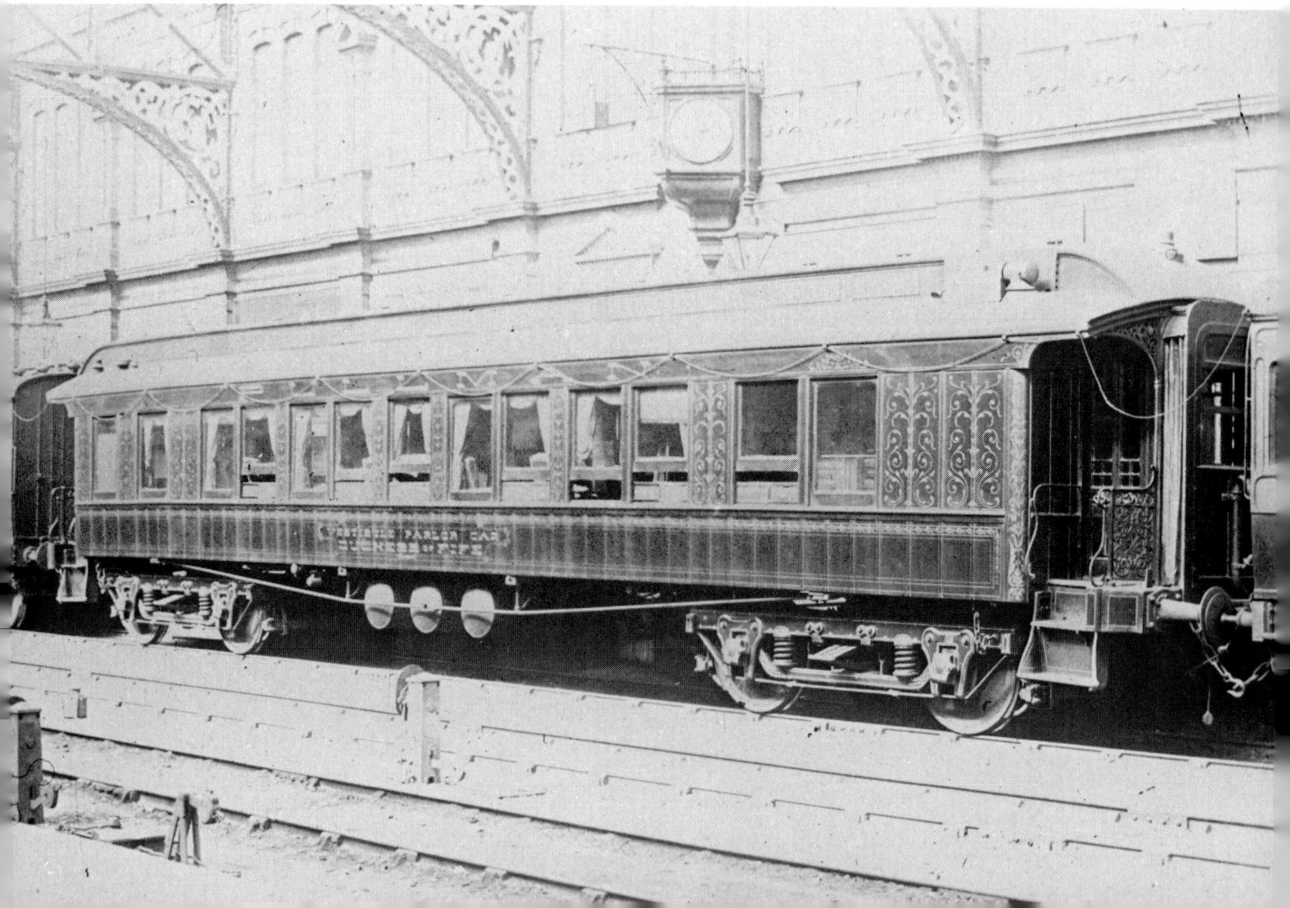

GOODS STOCK

Above: There were several types of South Western guards vans, No 5686 being of the large 24ton variety with sand-assisted braking./*Author's collection*

Below: For branch-line service there were 15 guards vans with side doors for the conveyance of parcels, No 44 being built at Eastleigh in 1911. /*Author's collection*

L S W R
9101
6-18-2
Load 12 Tons.

L S W R
12213
TARE. 13-15-1
Load 25 Tons.

ENGINEER'S DEPT
L S W R
500
TARE 17-4-1
LOAD 40 TONS

Top left: The standard tarpaulin bar 12ton goods wagon with side doors and spiral springing. /*Author's collection*

Centre left: Built experimentally in 1899 for the Southampton Docks brick trade, No 12213 proved liable to derail in sidings and was not repeated. /*British Railways*

Bottom left: Engineer's department 40ton ballast hopper with vacuum brake and diamond-framed bogies. No 500 was one of 20 built by C R Turner Ltd in 1904-11./*Author's collection*

Above: Over 800 of these covered wagons were built for general merchandise at Eastleigh between 1898 and Grouping./*Author's collection*

Below: Refrigerator van No 12626, with 269 others, was built for the Smithfield frozen meat traffic. All were painted salmon pink and many had vacuum and Westinghouse brakes./*Author's collection*

ACHILLE SERRE
MATCHLESS

SOUTH WESTERN
725
RAILWAY

STAFF

Left: Posed outside the parcels office at Bournemouth West in April 1902, the staff are recorded for posterity by the camera of C H Eden.

Far left, bottom: Drivers Bullard and Bartlett of Nine Elms proudly stand below the brass numberplate of 'Greyhound' No 725 at Bournemouth Central in January 1903./*C H Eden*

Below left: With their mantle of authority temporarily cast aside, two travelling ticket inspectors condescend to be photographed at Brockenhurst in June 1904./*C H Eden*

Right: The front end of T9 class No 702 and Driver Patterson at Bournemouth West in September 1905. /*C H Eden*

Below: The carriage piloting staff of two shunters and two porter-shunters at Bournemouth West in June 1903./*C H Eden*

ADAMS LOCOMOTIVES

Top left: Adams 46 class No 123 on the Nine Elms turntable in March 1881. Known as the 'Ironclads', these 4-4-0 tanks were delivered by Beyer Peacock & Co in 1879./*Ian Allan Library*

Centre left: In traffic the bunker capacity of the 'Ironclads' proved insufficient; therefore in 1883-6 all were rebuilt as 4-4-2 tanks like No 377.

Bottom left: The 46 class shortcomings led Adams to design the 415 class, of which 71 were built between 1882 and 1885. Here, No 417 stands between trains at Bournemouth Central in August 1902./*C H Eden*

Above: 415 class No 427 bustles through Stockbridge with a local train for Southampton in September 1901. /*Author's collection*

Below: In later years Adams preferred front-coupled passenger tanks and in 1888 introduced the T1s for suburban service. No 364 belonged to the final series and for a time ran with a Drummond spark arrester and conical smokebox door./*Author's collection*

Above: Smaller than the T1s, the O2 class mainly worked in the provinces, although a few, like No 232, were to be found around London./*Author's collection*

Below: Class 02 No 185 decorated and named *Alexandra* for the opening of the Bisley branch by the Princess of Wales in July 1890./*Author's collection*

Top right: The standard Adams six-coupled yard shunter, G6 class No 257, which had many details in common with the O2 class passenger tanks. /*E W Fry's collection*

Centre right: The Midhurst-Petersfield line in June 1908 with O2 class No 209 in charge of the branch services./*Author's collection*

Bottom right: G6 class No 263 working empty stone wagons into Easton station on the Isle of Portland in August 1901./*C H Eden*

L S W R
257

Above: B4 class four-coupled tank No 81 *Jersey* painted dark green and fitted with a canopy cab before transfer to the Docks Department at Southampton. /*Author's collection*

Below: 445 class No 448 at Nine Elms in October 1894, one of twelve elegant seven-foot 4-4-0s supplied by Robert Stephenson & Co in 1883 for the Salisbury and Southampton expresses.

Above: Basingstoke in May 1888, with 445 class No 446 running trials as a compound with 18in high and 24in low pressure cylinders./*Author's collection*

Below: In later days 445 class No 446 with a Drummond boiler, dome top lock-up safety valves and a lipped chimney.

467

L S W R

Top left: For the steeply graded Salisbury-Exeter line, Adams reduced the wheel diameter of his 4-4-0s to 6ft 7in. However their appearance, as exhibited by 460 class No 467, was not impaired and they remained neat and attractive.

Centre left: 460 class No 469 passing the new running shed buildings at Bournemouth Central with a semi-fast from Weymouth in June 1901./*C H Eden*

Bottom left: At speed between Bournemouth and Poole in September 1903, 460 class No 474 with its handsome Adams stove pipe replaced by a Drummond chimney./*Ian Allan Library*

Above: In early Drummond livery, 460 class No 526 proudly displays plaques commemorating its exhibition by Robert Stephenson & Co at Newcastle in 1886./*Author's collection*

Below: Mixed traffic 380 class 4-4-0 No 388 on Nine Elms shed in March 1901./*C H Eden*

Above: In later years Adams preferred 0-4-2s for mixed traffic service and in 1887-95 built the 90 'Jubilees'. No 534 is seen here about to leave Salisbury for Templecombe in September 1896./J B N Ashford

Below: The standard Adams goods locomotive, 395 class No 515, before delivery by the makers, Nielson & Co. of Glasgow./*Mitchell Library*

Top right: 'Jubilee' No 537 passing New Milton with a Bournemouth goods in September 1922. The neat stovepipe chimney has given way to one of Drummond pattern./*British Railways*

Centre right: Although employing the vacuum brake the South Western had a number of locomotives, including 'Jubilee' No 555, dual-fitted to cater for 'foreign' Westinghouse stock./*Author's collection*

L S W R
537

555
L S W R

LSWR
584
L S W R

No 579

Top left: X2 class No 584 at Nine Elms in April 1895. These later day Adams 7ft 1in 4-4-0s performed as excellently as they looked.

Centre left: Esher in September 1904, with X2 class No 579 approaching with a Portsmouth express. /*Ian Allan Library*

Bottom left: The luxury of double-heading was not a Drummond indulgence, so the photographer was fortunate to find T3 No 574 and X6 No 659 leaving Salisbury with an up express in July 1906. /*Loco & General*

Above: Undoubtedly the best known of all Adams locomotives, T3 class No 563, now a resident of the National Railway Museum, York.

Below: T6 class No 680 near St. Cross with a Waterloo-Bournemouth Pullman car express on 19 August 1901./*C H Eden*

WIMBLEDON
260
No 682

Left: By Grouping the Adams express classes had long been relegated to minor duties. Here, T6 class No 682 passes Wimbledon with a Basingstoke semi-fast in May 1925./*H C Casserley*

Above: Driver Webb and his fireman pose on board immaculately-groomed T6 class No 682 at Bournemouth West on 7 August 1902./*C H Eden*

Below: For many years a familiar sight on the South Western, X6 class No 664 at Oatlands heading the 2.25pm Wimbledon-Templecombe milk vans on 11 May 1912./*LCGB*

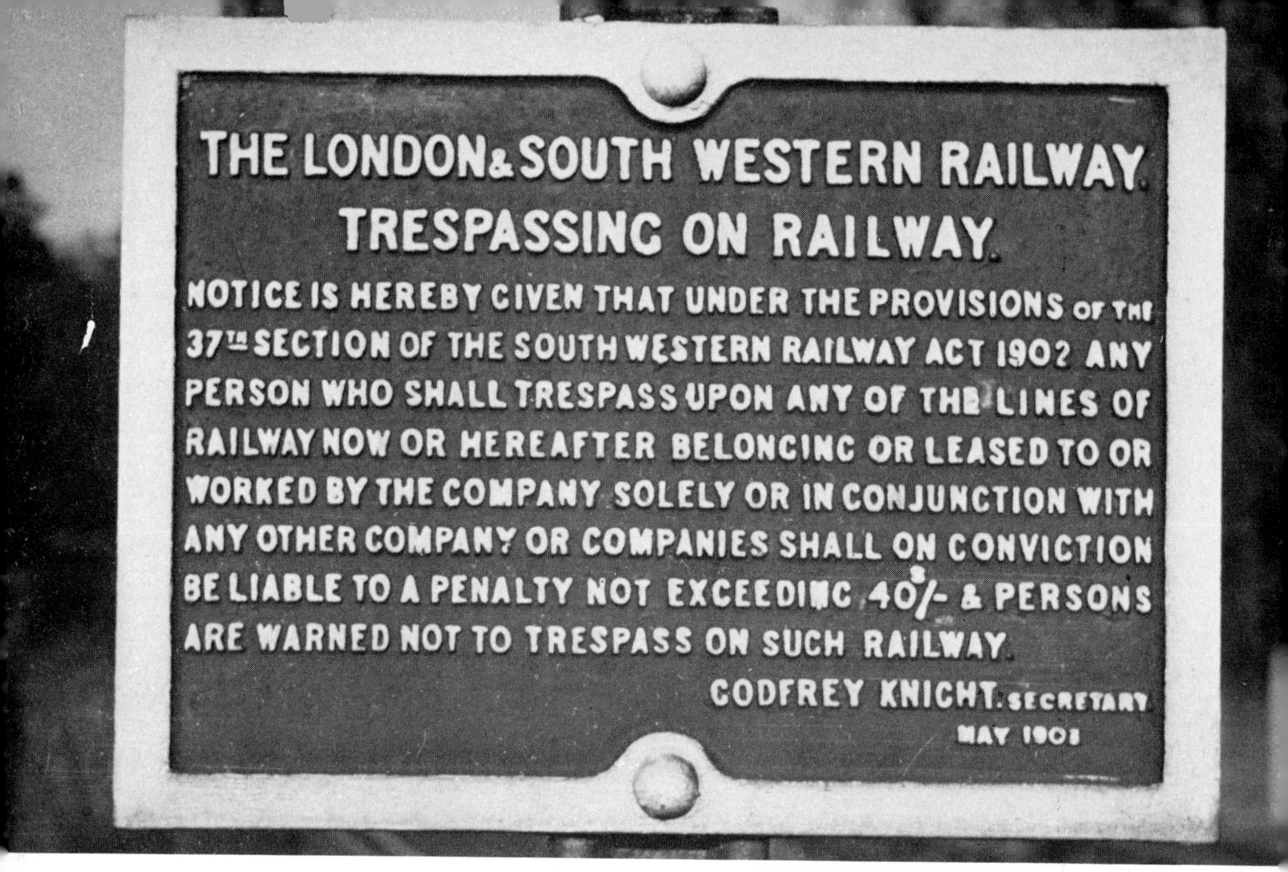
THE LONDON & SOUTH WESTERN RAILWAY
TRESPASSING ON RAILWAY
NOTICE IS HEREBY GIVEN THAT UNDER THE PROVISIONS OF THE 37TH SECTION OF THE SOUTH WESTERN RAILWAY ACT 1902 ANY PERSON WHO SHALL TRESPASS UPON ANY OF THE LINES OF RAILWAY NOW OR HEREAFTER BELONGING OR LEASED TO OR WORKED BY THE COMPANY SOLELY OR IN CONJUNCTION WITH ANY OTHER COMPANY OR COMPANIES SHALL ON CONVICTION BE LIABLE TO A PENALTY NOT EXCEEDING 40s/- & PERSONS ARE WARNED NOT TO TRESPASS ON SUCH RAILWAY.
GODFREY KNIGHT. SECRETARY
MAY 1903

L.& S.W.R.
TRESPASSERS
WILL BE
PROSECUTED

L.& S.W.R.
DANGER.
DON'T TOUCH
CONDUCTOR RAILS.

SIGNS

Left: This cast plate, typical of many on the South Western system, was located at Cooks Crossing, Oxshott, and was always maintained in excellent condition./*R F Roberts*

Far left, bottom: Equally indestructible were the cast trespassers notices, this example being sited at Hampton Court Junction./*R F Roberts*

Below left: The self-explanatory vitreous-enamelled electrification notice at Claygate/*R F Roberts*

Above: The plaque commemorating the opening of Central Bridge, Southampton in July 1882./*E W Fry*

Below: The gradient posts were generally of wood with arms of cast iron, this example being at Claygate. /*E W Fry*

Right: The ¾mile post at Malden mounted on a concrete boundary post./*R F Roberts*

LONDON & SOUTH WESTERN RAILWAY C^OY
563
NINE ELMS WORKS 1893

ODDMENTS

IRONSIDE

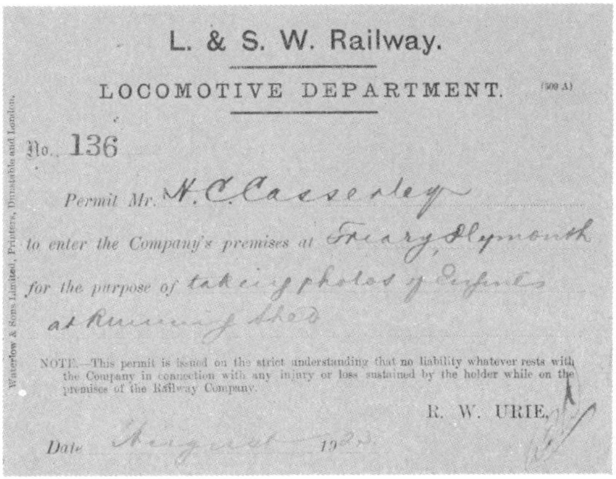

L. & S. W. Railway.

LOCOMOTIVE DEPARTMENT. (509 A)

No. 136

Permit Mr. H. C. Casserley

to enter the Company's premises at Friary, Plymouth

for the purpose of taking photos of [illegible] at Running Shed

NOTE.—This permit is issued on the strict understanding that no liability whatever rests with the Company in connection with any injury or loss sustained by the holder while on the premises of the Railway Company.

R. W. URIE.

Date August 19[illegible]

Waterlow & Sons Limited, Printers, Dunstable and London.

Far left, top: The numberplate of Adams T3 class 4-4-0 No 563 now preserved, together with the locomotive, at York./*E W Fry*

Far left, bottom: The neat nameplate of *Ironside*, a four-coupled Hawthorn, Leslie saddle tank obtained from the Southampton Dock Company in 1891./*D L Bradley*

Above: Beattie goods No 092 *Charon* was condemned in June 1906, but fortunately one nameplate was preserved to reach Clapham and now York./*E W Fry*

Above left: A familiar document in recent years, but a rarity before grouping.

Left: Ironside's numberplate, the line below denoting relegation to the Duplicate List./*H C Casserley*

ROAD VEHICLES

Above: A Clarkson steam bus at Nine Elms in May 1905. Four were purchased for the Exeter-Chagford and New Milton-Lymington services, but did not prove successful and were sold in 1908. /*Author's collection*

Left: Thorneycroft petrol bus AA 2187 near Hindhead en route from Farnham to Haslemere in July 1908./*Photomatic*

Below left: Parcel delivering at Woking before the motor-age./*Author's collection*

MISCELLANEOUS LOCOMOTIVES

Above: Mr Drummond's Car, built in 1899 to provide transport to and from Nine Elms Works as well as rapid and surreptitious inspection of the line. /*Author's collection*

Below: Southampton Dock Company 0-4-0 saddle tank *Vulcan* at Poole in May 1902. Built by the Vulcan Foundry in 1878, it entered LSWR stock in 1891 and was sold in 1924./*C H Eden*

Right: Manning Wardle 0-6-0 saddle tank No 458 *Jumbo.* Obtained second-hand in 1883, it was employed on the isolated Bodmin & Wadebridge line until withdrawal in 1896./*Author's collection*

Far right: 'Terrier' in unfamiliar surroundings, No 646 *Newington* purchased with No 668 *Clapham* in March 1903 for the sharply-graded and curved Lyme Regis branch./*Author's collection*

Below: The Royal Pier, Southampton in June 1894 with Alexander Shanks 0-4-0 saddle tank No 109 *Southampton* on arrival from the Terminus station./*Author's collection*

NEWINGTON
646

GOLD MEDAL.
RANDALL, SLOPER & C^os.
MINERAL WATERS.
100
BUILDING
SITES
SOAP

Above: Plymouth, Devonport & South Western Junction Railway 0-6-2 tank *Earl of Mount Edgcumbe* at Eastleigh as South Western No 757 in October 1923./*E W Fry's collection*

Below: Bodmin, a small 0-4-0 saddle tank built by Fletcher, Jennings & Co in 1864 for the Bodmin & Wadebridge line./*Author's collection*

SIGNAL BOXES

Above: Around London gantry signalboxes were a feature of the South Western. Often in the early years they were topped by signals, like this box outside Waterloo./*Author's collection*

Left: Cooks Crossing, Oxshott, typical of many wayside signal boxes controlling level crossings. /*R F Roberts*

Below left: The tall brick and timber structure of the Sidmouth Junction box was employed where elevation was necessary to provide signalmen with an unobstructed view of the line./*R F Roberts*

Below: Strawberry Hill, showing the neat junction signalbox, co-acting signals and crossing gates. /*Author's collection*

SIGNALS

This picture: The up starting signals at Bournemouth Central in June 1902 with T6 class No 677 entering the down platform on a Waterloo express./*C H Eden*

Right: The neat pattern ground shunt signal used by the South Western for many years, some surviving until the end of steam./*E W Fry*

Far right: The down main-line starting signal at Sidmouth Junction with co-acting arms mounted on a tall lattice post./*R F Roberts*

Below right: A fixed distant signal on a wooden post near Sidmouth Junction, on the branch line to Sidmouth./*R F Roberts*

Below, far right: The South Western had responsibility for signalling on the Somerset & Dorset Joint Railway, hence the appearance of these signals at Midford./*E W Fry*

Right: An unusual signal with slotted arm at Esher Race Course station./*R F Roberts*

Below: Superheated D15 class No 471 heads a Waterloo express below an impressive array of track circuit-controlled automatic signals near Woking. /*H C Casserley*

DRUMMOND LOCOMOTIVES

Above: By 1895 singles had regained favour, consequently Drummond's initial express design sought their free running without abandoning all the advantages of coupled wheels. The result, T7 class double-single No 720, is seen here at Bournemouth West in September 1900./*C H Eden*

Below: No 720, with the larger 1905 boiler, heads the 11.00am West of England express through Earlsfield in August 1911./*Ian Allan Library*

Above: The 1901 E10 class double-singles, Nos 369 to 373, were similar to No 720 before reboilering, and like this engine seldom performed as well as the Drummond 4-4-0s./*Author's collection*

Below: C8 class No 297 passing Swaythling at speed with a Waterloo-Bournemouth express in March 1899. Only ten of these neat 4-4-0s were built before Drummond introduced the larger T9s. /*Author's collection*

Top right: The most renowned Drummond class, T9 No 728 pauses briefly at Brockenhurst with the 9.30am Waterloo-Bournemouth express in July 1901./*C H Eden*

Centre right: T9 class No 702 at Bournemouth West in August 1902. Because of their fine turn of speed and free running the men knew these excellent 4-4-0s as the 'Greyhounds'./*C H Eden*

Bottom right: Lord Kitchener's train and T9 class No 773 at Southampton on 12 July 1902. Standing on the track are Locomotive Inspectors Wilkinson and Moore, and Driver James of Nine Elms./*C H Eden*

L S W R

L S W R

K

773
L S W R

285

Top left: A down West of England restaurant car express approaching Esher, headed by T9 class No 300 in May 1908./*Ian Allan Library*

Centre left: Robert Urie superheated many of the Drummond classes, but none so successfully as the T9s; No 773 is seen at Plymouth Friary in July 1924./*H C Casserley*

Bottom left: Superheated T9 No 314 passing Esher with a White Star boat express in September 1923. /*Ian Allan Library*

Above: An impressive view of 700 class goods No 680 at Salisbury in July 1896. The conical smokebox door denotes the incorporation of a Drummond spark arrester./*J B Ashford*

Right: Under easy steam 700 class No 459 passes St. Cross with a Southampton goods in August 1901. /*C H Eden*

32

700

166
L S W R

Top left: A Boer War troop special in charge of 700 class No 687 passes Northam with the South Staffordshire Regiment in October 1899. /*Author's collection*

Centre left: Like other Drummond classes, the 700 goods were greatly improved by superheating. Just back from Eastleigh Works No 700 prepares to leave Nine Elms shed in April 1923./*H C Casserley*

Bottom left: In 1901-7 Drummond built 80 small-wheeled 4-4-0s of classes K10 and L11 for mixed traffic duties. No 166 featured here is of the larger L11 class./*Author's collection*

Above: M7 class No 108 in February 1904. Over 100 of these large 0-4-4 tanks were built by Drummond for suburban and secondary main line service. /*Author's collection*

Below: Framed by a footbridge between Epsom and Ashtead, M7 class No 321 accelerates past with a Guildford train in August 1921./*C H Housego*

L S W R
126

Nº 397

395
L S W R

Top left: Urie superheated M7 No 126 in July 1921, but to such small advantage that no others were similarly modified./*Author's collection*

Centre left: S11 class No 397 leaving Waterloo with an Exeter express in April 1907. Ten of these 6ft 1in 4-4-0s were introduced in 1903 for service over the heavily graded West of England line.
/*Author's collection*

Bottom left: Under Drummond's superintendency the preparation of locomotives for royal occasions attained its peak. Here, S11 class No 395 awaits the visit of President Joubert to Farnborough in July 1903./*Author's collection*

Above: The L12 class of 1904-5 was similar to the S11s apart from having 6ft 7in coupled wheels. No 433 stands at Plymouth North Road in May 1911./*Ian Allan Library*

Below: L12 class No 434 in all its glory at Nine Elms for the state visit of King Alphonso XIII of Spain.
/*Author's collection*

No 432
L S W R

L S W R
471

333
L S W

Top left: Superheated L12 No 432 passes Earlsfield with a West of of England express in July 1921. */Ian Allan Library*

Centre left: Drummond's finale, the magnificent D15 class 4-4-0s of 1912. No 471 stands outside Eastleigh Works awaiting despatch to service. */Author's collection*

Left: F13 No 333 prepares to leave Exeter in September 1906. Five of these massive 4-cylinder 4-6-0s were built by Drummond in 1905 for the West of England expresses.*/Loco & General*

Top: Superheating was a needless complication to Drummond, but Urie appreciated its value and in 1915-7 equipped the D15s. No 470 awaits signals at Salisbury in March 1921.*/E W Fry's collection*

Above: The only one of the species, E14 class No 335. Supposedly a modified F13, but experience proved it the least successful of all the Drummond 4-6-0s. */Author's collection*

448

Left: An up Exeter Breakfast Car express in the charge of G14 class No 457. Smaller and more versatile than the F13s, the class worked the West of England services until Grouping./*Ian Allan Library*

Below left: F13 class No 334 leaving Salisbury with a Southampton goods in April 1914, services to which the class was relegated after failing in an express role. /*LCGB*

Bottom left: P14 class No 448 at Eastleigh in March 1911, a variation of the G14s which gave similar excellent service west of Salisbury.

Below: T14 class No 461 when new. Because of their massive splashers, the men referred to them as the 'Paddleboxes'.

Bottom: Scant regard was shown by the Southern Railway for the Drummond 4-6-0s and all were hurriedly withdrawn except the T14s. Here G14 No 456 awaits breaking up at Eastleigh in June 1925./*Real Photos*

Above: Eastleigh in July 1915, with T14 class No 444 passing with a Bournemouth express, services on which they excelled until Grouping.
/Author's collection

Superheated T14 No 447 thunders through Earlsfield with a Bournemouth express in June 1922.
/Real Photos

WORKS

Above: Beattie 2-4-0 No 121 *St George* being dismantled at Nine Elms in February 1898. */Ian Allan Library*

Below: Adams T3 class 6ft 7in 4-4-0 No 573 under construction at Nine Elms in August 1893. */Author's collection*

0373

Above left: Nine Elms yards in February 1903 with single-frame goods No 0373 awaiting breaking up. /*C H Eden*

Left: The first Drummond 4-6-0, F13 class No 330, being assembled at Nine Elms in August 1905. The man-hole covers conceal the cross water tubes. /*Author's collection*

Above: C14 class No 736 at Nine Elms in September 1906. Apparently no decision on the siting of the numerals had been made for they appear in chalk on both tank and bunker sides./*Author's collection*

Below: F13 class No 333 awaits final attention in the Erecting Shop at Nine Elms before transfer to the Paint Shop./*Author's collection*

Above: Nine Elms ceased operation at the end of 1909 to be replaced by a more spacious establishment at Eastleigh. Where D15 class No 472 nears completion in December 1912 with Jubilee No 598 and X6 class No 665 returning to traffic after overhaul. /*Author's collection*

Below: T1 class 0-4-4 tank No 1 and X2 class 4-4-0 No 583 under repair at Eastleigh Works in June 1924./*H C Casserley*

RAIL CARS

Top & above: The East Southsea branch was jointly operated with the LB&SCR using tank locomotives and coaches until mid-1903 when Drummond introduced two steam railcars. These two views show the front and rear of Joint Car No 1 at Eastleigh Carriage Works in April 1903./*C H Eden*

Below: Joint Car No 2 at Fratton in August 1903 after the enlargement of its vertical boiler. /*Author's collection*

Above: Later Drummond constructed steam railcars for service on the South Western. Here, H12 class No 2 stops at Cliddesden on the Basingstoke-Alton Line in August 1906./*Loco & General*

Below: H13 class No 10 at Padstow in 1906. This final series had the engine unit incorporated with the coach giving a more neat appearance./*Loco & General*

Above: In service the railcars proved so inflexible that by 1907 most had been displaced by 2-2-0 tanks and trailer cars. C14 class No 736, painted grey for the official photographer, is seen here at Nine Elms in September 1906./*Author's collection*

Below: Unfortunately, the C14s suffered similar limitation and in turn were replaced. Most were then laid aside until sold to the Government in 1916-7. However, four, like No 741, were rebuilt as four-coupled shunters./*H C Casserley*

RUNNING SHEDS

Top left: Rebuilt Beattie 6ft 6in 2-4-0 No 21 posed at Nine Elms on Sunday 23 September 1897 with the shed foreman and his staff./*Author's collection*

Centre left: North Devon Railway broad gauge 2-4-0 *Creedy* on the turntable outside Barnstaple repair shops in April 1877, the date of its withdrawal. /*Author's collection*

Left: The new running shed at Bournemouth Central in July 1896 with 'Vesuvius' class 2-4-0 No 294 stopped for attention./*Author's collection*

Top: The interior of Salisbury shed in August 1906 displaying a commendable degree of order and cleanliness./*Author's collection*

Above: Jubilees Nos 535 and 652, and 135 class No 143 in residence at the old shed Bournemouth Central in August 1902./*C H Eden*

Above: Eastleigh shed on Sunday 15 April 1922, the engines nearest the camera being Nos 91, 0111 *Vulcan* and 0458 *Ironside*./*H. C. Casserley*

Below: Rebuilt Beyer Peacock double-frame goods No 277A at the coal stage, Strawberry Hill, in October 1921./*H C Casserley*

SCENES: CLAPHAM JUNCTION

Above: Looking west with the Brighton station on the left, X6 class No 660 is passing through with an up express and an M7 stands on the Windsor line below the signal box. /*Ian Allan Library*

Below: Looking towards Waterloo with L12 class No 419 approaching on a West of England express and a radial tank coming off the West London Extension./*Ian Allan Library*

ACCIDENTS

Above: T6 class No 684 awaits repair in March 1903 after breaking a coupling rod near Worplesdon with a Portsmouth express./*C H Eden*

Below: Drummond goods No 700 at Nine Elms in October 1900 after having its front buffer beam, near side coupling rod and cab footsteps buckled by a platelayers trolley at Worcester Park. /*Author's collection*

Top: M7 class No 58 displaying evidence of its collision with a rake of coal wagons at Guildford in May 1904./*Author's collection*

Above: The aftermath of the Salisbury derailment; Beyer Peacock double-frame goods No 0351 awaiting repair at Nine Elms in July 1906./*Author's collection*

URIE LOCOMOTIVES

Above: H15 class No 486 outside Eastleigh Works in January 1914, the first of Robert Urie's two-cylinder mixed traffic 4-6-0s./*Author's collection*

Right: On all counts the robustly constructed H15s outpaced the Drummond classes. In this view No 482 is seen approaching Earlsfield with a Bournemouth express in August 1914./*Real Photos*

Below: N15 class No 743 at Axminster in March 1919. After Grouping these fine-looking express 4-6-0s were developed into the successful 'King Arthur' class./*Loco & General*

Top: In the first summer of Grouping, N15 class No 741 storms through Earlsfield at the head of a West of England express./*Ian Allan Library*

Above: Still to receive its Southern Railway livery, N15 class No 754 stands on Bournemouth Central shed in May 1925./*H. C. Casserley*

Above: S15 class 4-6-0 No 506 at Nine Elms in October 1921. This goods derivative of the N15s possessed such an excellent turn of speed that it was frequently pressed into express service. */Author's collection*

Left: A heavy Nine Elms Yard-Bournemouth goods in the charge of S15 class No 501.*/Loco & General*

Below: Like the 4-6-0s Urie built his tank classes large and powerful. Here, H16 4-6-2 tank No 516 makes an imposing sight when new in November 1921. */Author's collection*

BRIDGES

Above: The graceful columns of Meldon Viaduct photographed from the north side looking east. */E W Fry*

Below: Adams O2 class No 218 crossing the Plym swing bridge with a Turnchapel train in July 1924. */H C Casserley*

Above: Holsworthy East Viaduct on the Bude branch in September 1923./*LCGB*

Below: A neat three-span girder bridge over the River Camel near Padstow./*Photomatic*